Mary

Mother
of my Lord

Mary

MOTHER OF MY LORD

CHRISTINE GRANGER

NOVALIS
THE LITURGICAL PRESS
THE COLUMBA PRESS

For Sebastian

Credits:

Cover: Eye-to-Eye Design
Interior Design and Layout: Christiane Lemire, Francine Petitclerc
Editor: Bernadette Gasslein

Paintings © Christine Granger. No painting may be reproduced without the written permission of the artist.

© 1996.

Novalis, Saint Paul University, Ottawa, Ontario, Canada
Business Office: Novalis, 49 Front Street East, 2nd floor,
Toronto, Ontario M5E 1B3
ISBN 2-89088-784-7 (soft cover)
ISBN 2-89-88-813-4 (hard cover)

The Liturgical Press, Saint John's Abbey, Collegeville, Minnesota USA 56321
ISBN 08146 2466-9

The Columba Press, 55 A Spruce Avenue, Stillorgan Industrial Park,
Blackrock, Dublin, Ireland.
ISBN 1-85607-187-1

Canadian Cataloguing in Publication Data

Granger, Christine, 1941-
  Mary, Mother of My Lord

ISBN 2-89088-784-7

  1. Granger, Christine, 1941- 2. Mary, Blessed Virgin, Saint—Art. 3. Mary, Blessed Virgin, Saint—Prayer-books and devotions-English. I. Title.

N8070.G73 1996   759.11   C96-900768-X

All right reserved. No part of this book may be reproduced, stored in a retrieval system, or transmitted, in any form or by any means, electronic, mechanical, photocopying, recording, or otherwise, without prior written permission from the publishers.

Printed and bound in Canada.

I was taught
that every contemplative soul
to whom it is given to look and to seek
will see Mary
and pass on to God
through contemplation.

Julian of Norwich

Contents

Introduction	9
Mary	11

Traditional Prayers

Act of Consecration	13
In Your Care	15
Hail Mary	17
Angelus	19
Magnificat	21
Hail, Holy Queen	25
Memorare	27
Regina Caeli	29
Prayer to Our Lady of Lourdes	31
Prayer to Our Lady of Guadalupe	33
Prayer to Our Lady of Fatima	35
The Rosary: Method	37
The Rosary: Mysteries	39
Litany of the Blessed Virgin Mary	41
Rejoice! (Akathistos Hymn)	49

Poetry

"Mary, Mother of Divine Grace *51*
Compared to the Air We Breathe"
Gerard Manley Hopkins
"Symphonia" (excerpt) *55*
Hildegard of Bingen

Hymns

O First-Born Daughter *57*
Immaculate Mary *59*
O Sanctissima *61*

Notes *62*

Afterword: The Paintings *63*

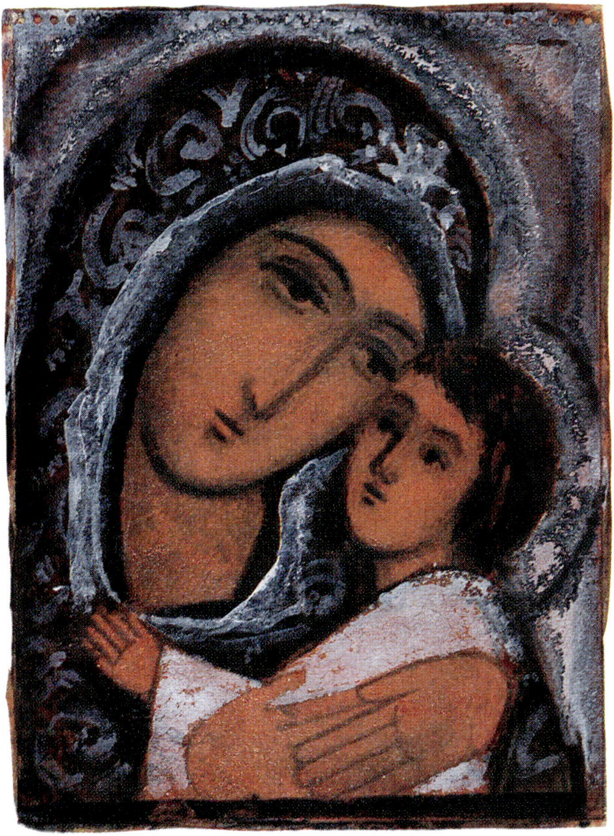

Introduction

We feel your love around us, Mary,
in every time and place and age.
We come to you,
We bless you,
We praise you.
O Mother of God,
you are the greatest of saints,
the holiest of human beings,
the gentlest and loveliest
of God's creatures.
Mother of grace,
our Mother.

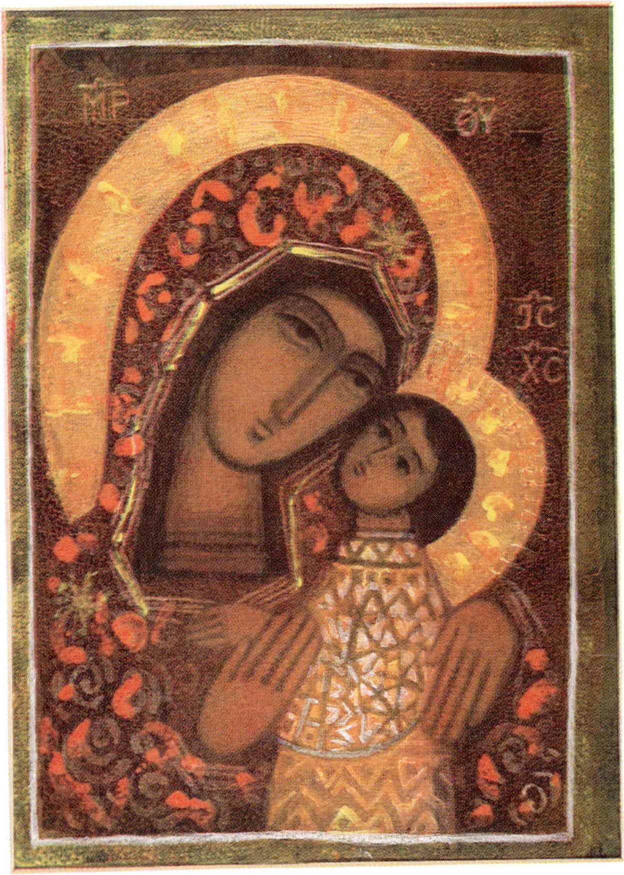
ΜΡ
ΘΥ
ΙϹ
ΧϹ

Mary

Blessed the womb that sheltered him.
Blessed the eyes that beheld him.
Blessed the hands that held him.
Blessed the lips that kissed him.
Blessed the feet that walked with him.
Blessed are you among women.
The chosen one of all creation,
chosen before all time
for all time
to be God-bearer:
the Mother of Jesus Christ
our Redeemer.

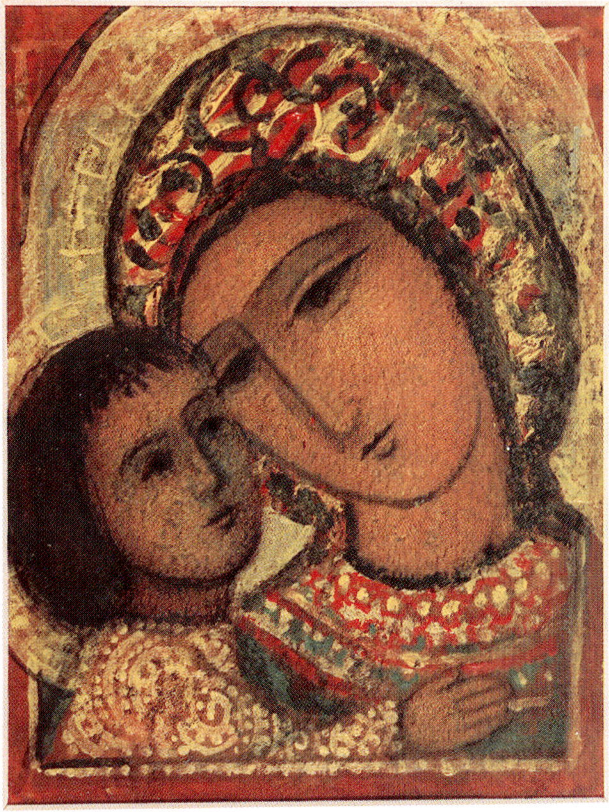

Act of Consecration

Mary, my mother,
I consecrate myself
and all my days and
ways to you.
Safeguard me from
the enemy.
Let me live and grow
in Christ's love
which encompasses all
and surpasses all.

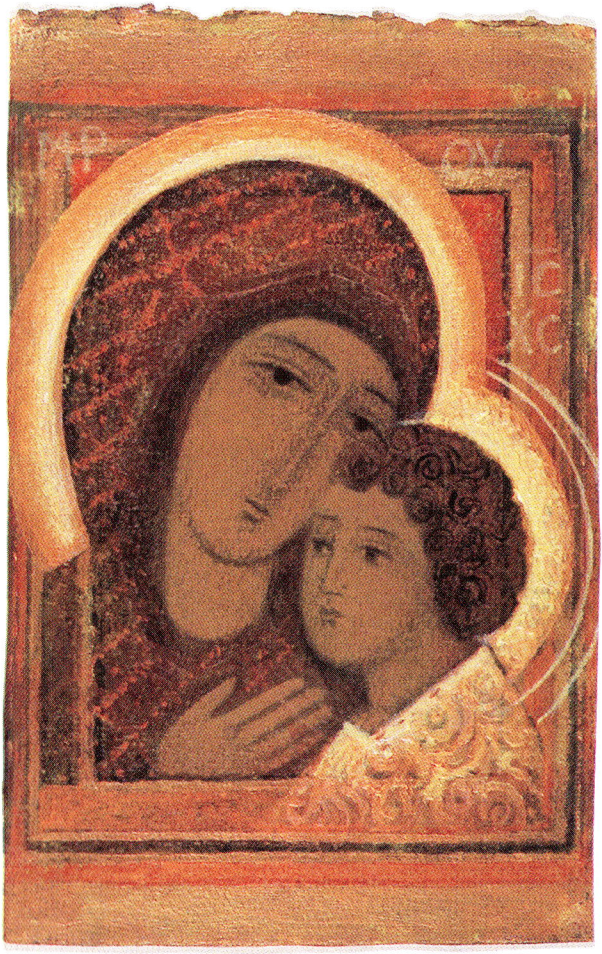
MP ΘΥ
IC XC

In Your Care

We run to you and place ourselves in your
care, O Virgin Mother of God.
Do not turn away
from our prayers and troubles,
but safeguard us from danger and misfortune,
immaculate and blessed lady.

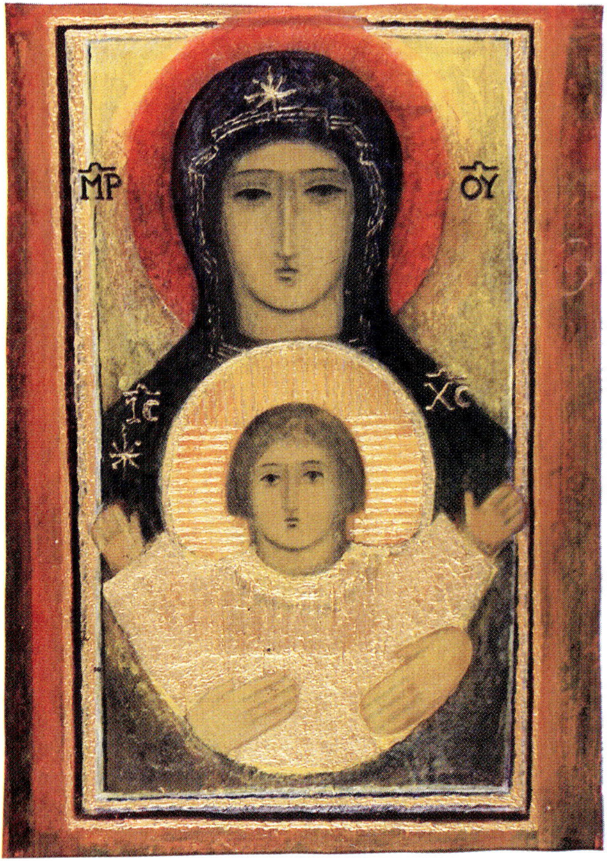
ΜΡ ΘΥ
ΙC ΧC

Hail Mary

Hail Mary, full of grace,
the Lord is with thee.
Blessed art thou among women
and blessed is the fruit of thy womb,
Jesus.
Holy Mary, Mother of God,
pray for us sinners,
now and at the hour of our death.
Amen.

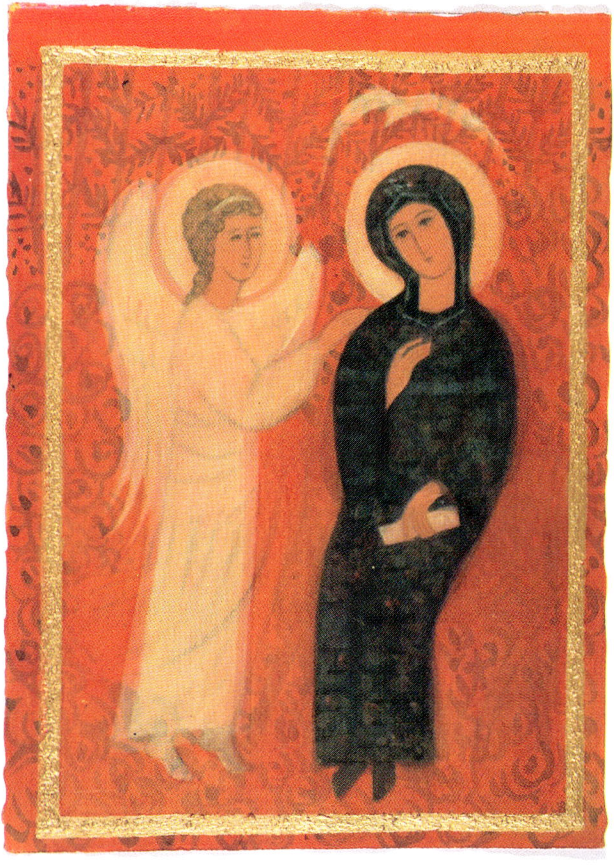

Angelus

The angel of the Lord declared unto Mary, and she conceived of the Holy Spirit.
Hail Mary ...

Behold, the handmaid of the Lord; be it done to me according to thy word.
Hail Mary ...

And the word was made flesh, and dwelt among us. *Hail Mary ...*

Pray for us, O holy Mother of God; that we may be made worthy of the promises of Christ.

Pour forth, we beseech thee, O Lord, thy grace into our hearts, that we to whom the message of thy Son was made known by an angel, may by his passion and death be brought to the glory of his resurrection, through the same Christ our Lord. Amen.

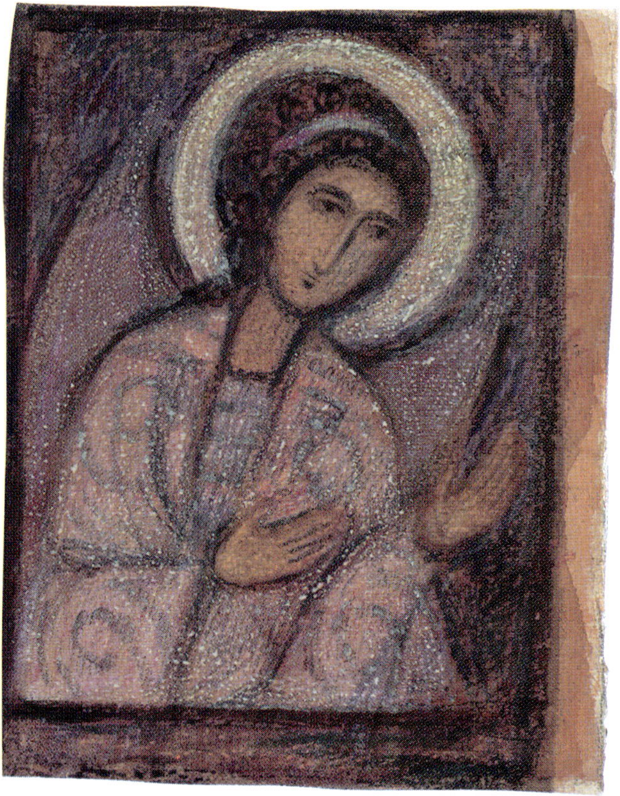

Magnificat

And Mary said:
"My soul magnifies the Lord
And my spirit rejoices in God my Saviour,
For he has looked with favour on the lowliness of his servant.
Surely, from now on all generations will call me blessed;
for the Mighty One has done great things for me; and holy is his name.
His mercy is for those who fear him
from generation to generation.

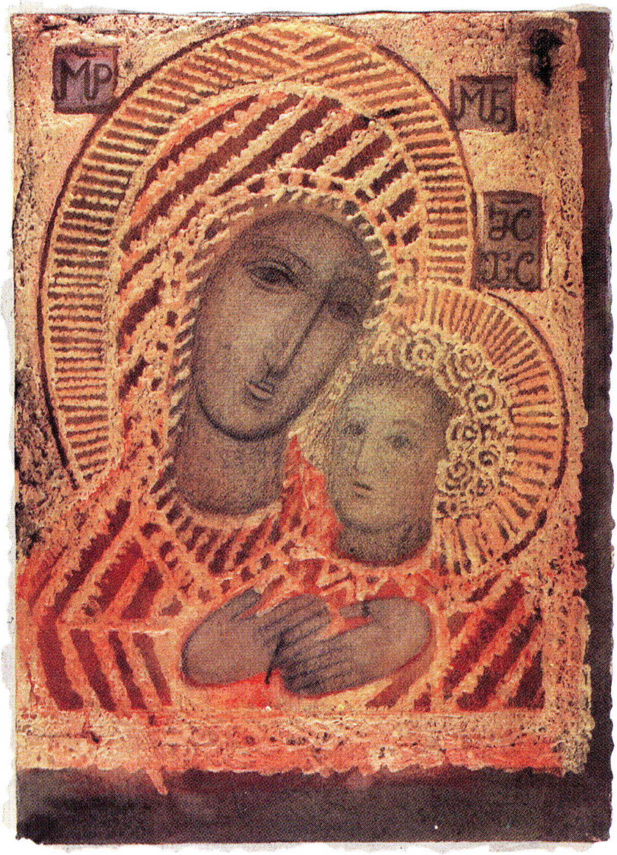

He has shown strength with his arm
he has scattered the proud in the thoughts
of their hearts.
He has brought down the powerful
from their thrones,
and lifted up the lowly;
he has filled the hungry with good things,
and sent the rich away empty.
He has helped his servant Israel,
in remembrance of his mercy,
according to the promise he made
to our ancestors,
to Abraham
and to his descendants forever."

Luke 1: 46-55

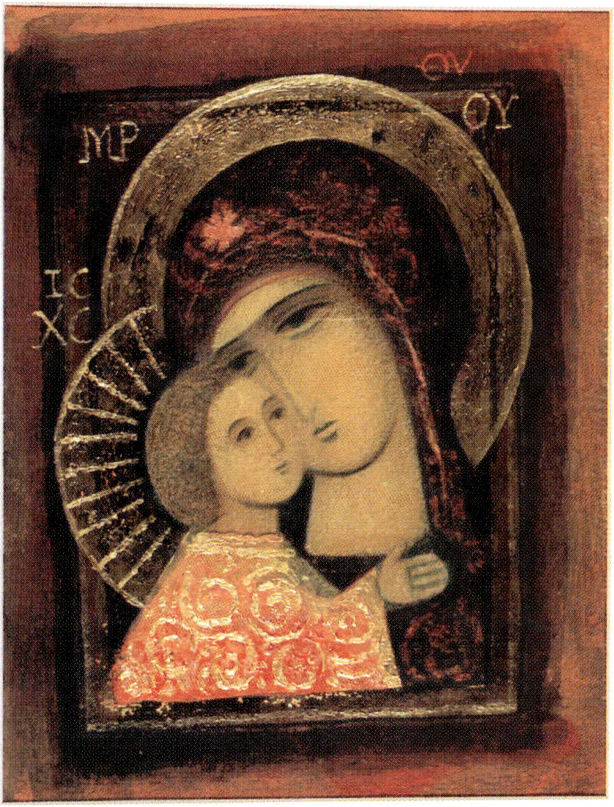
MP
IC
XC

Hail, Holy Queen

Hail, holy Queen, mother of mercy,
our life, our sweetness and our hope.
To you do we cry,
poor banished children of Eve.
To you we send up our sighs,
mourning and weeping
in this valley of tears.
Turn then, most gracious advocate,
your eyes of mercy upon us,
and after this, our exile,
show unto us the blessed fruit of your
womb, Jesus.
O clement, O loving,
O kind Virgin Mary.

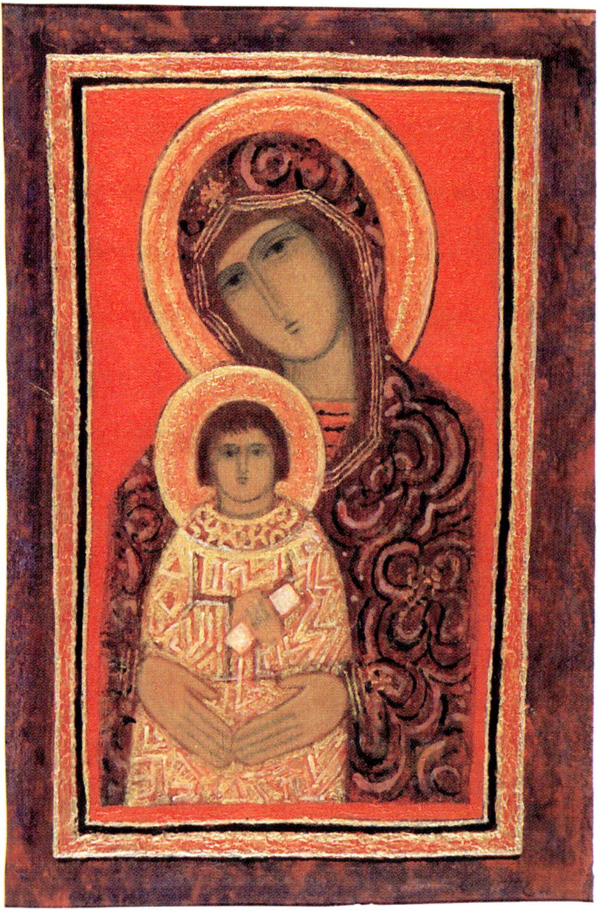

Memorare

Remember, most gracious Virgin Mary,
that never was it known that anyone who
fled to your protection,
implored your help,
and sought your intercession,
was left unaided.
Inspired with this confidence,
I fly to you,
O Virgin of virgins, my mother.
To you I come;
before you I stand, sinful and sorrowful.
Mother of the Word Incarnate,
despise not my petitions
but, in your mercy, hear and answer me.

St. Bernard of Clairvaux, 1090-1153

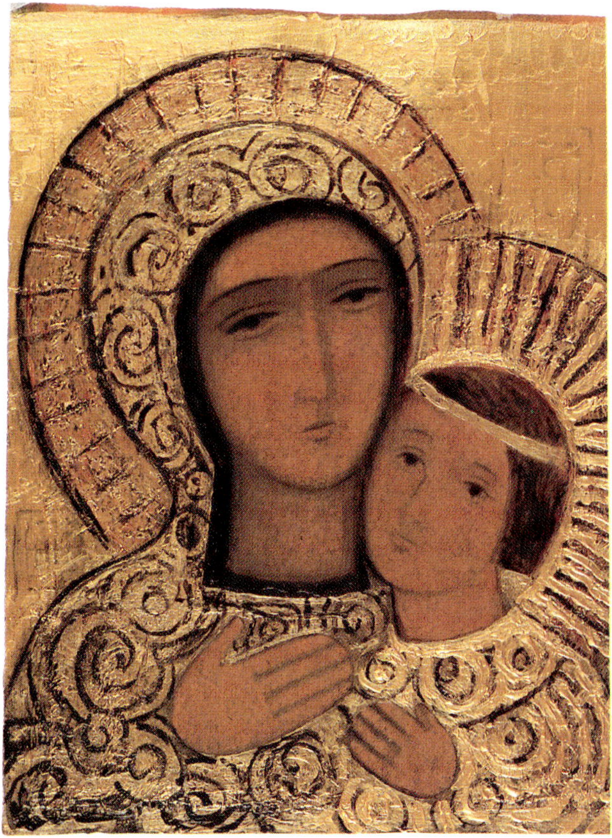

Regina Caeli

O Queen of heaven, rejoice, alleluia!
For he whom you chose to bear, alleluia!
Is risen as he said, alleluia!
Pray for us to God, alleluia!
Rejoice and be glad,
O Virgin Mary, alleluia!
For the Lord is truly risen, alleluia!
O God,
by the resurrection of your Son, our Lord,
you were pleased
to make glad the whole world.
Grant, we beseech you, that through the
intercession of the Virgin Mary, his mother,
we may attain the joys of everlasting life,
through the same Christ our Lord. Amen.

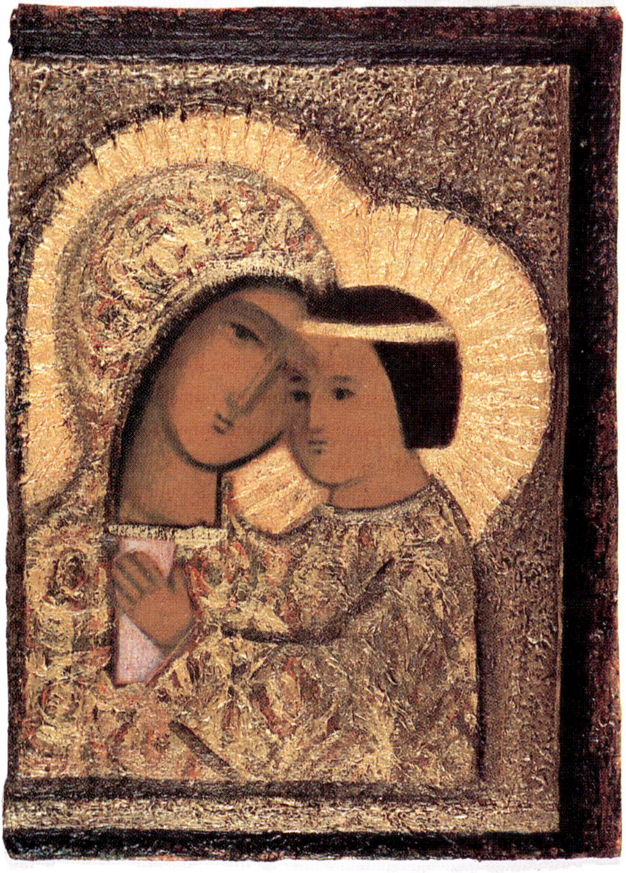

Our Lady of Lourdes

O Immaculate Virgin Mary,
you are the refuge of sinners,
the health of the sick,
and the comfort of the afflicted.
By your appearances at the Grotto of Lourdes,
you made it a privileged sanctuary
where your favours are given to people
streaming to it from the whole world.
Over the years countless sufferers
have obtained the cure of their infirmities—
whether of soul, mind or body.
Therefore I come with limitless confidence
to implore your motherly intercessions.
Loving Mother,
obtain the grant of my requests.
Let me strive to imitate your virtues on earth
so that I may one day share your glory in heaven.

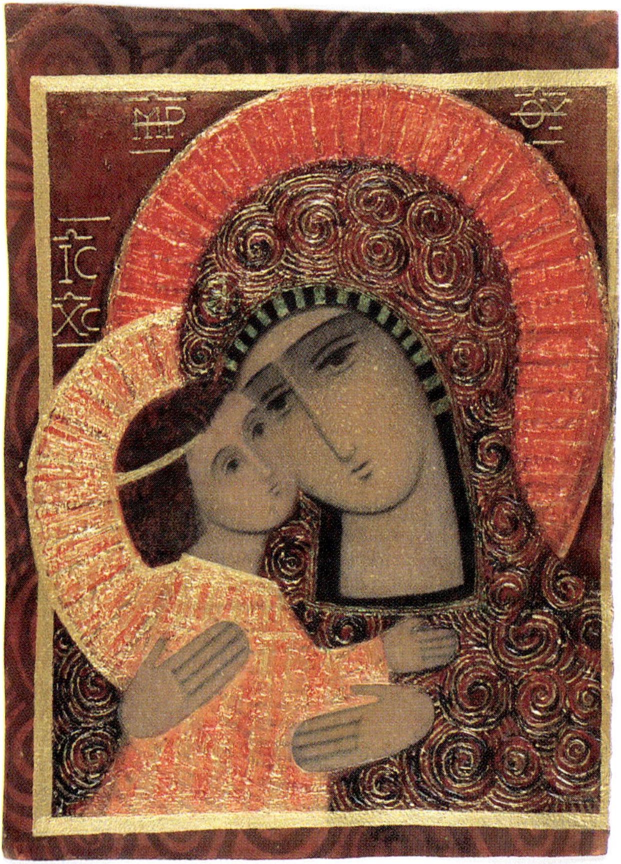
MP ΘY
IC XC

Our Lady of Guadalupe

Our Lady of Guadalupe,
mystical rose,
intercede for the Church,
protect the Holy Father,
help all who invoke you in their necessities.
Since you are the ever Virgin Mary
and Mother of the true God,
obtain for us from your most holy Son
the grace of a firm faith and a sure hope
amid the bitterness of life,
as well as an ardent love
and the precious gift of final perseverance.

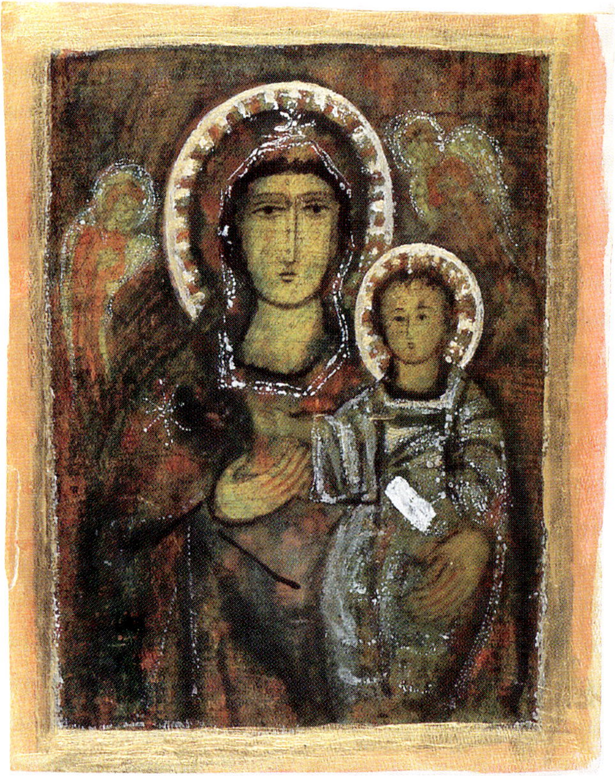

Our Lady of Fatima

O Most holy Virgin Mary,
Queen of the most holy Rosary,
you were pleased to appear
to the children of Fatima
and reveal a glorious message.
We implore you,
inspire in our hearts a fervent love
for the recitation of the Rosary.
By meditating on the mysteries
of the redemption
that are recalled therein
may we obtain the graces and virtues
that we ask,
through the merits of Jesus Christ,
our Lord and Redeemer.

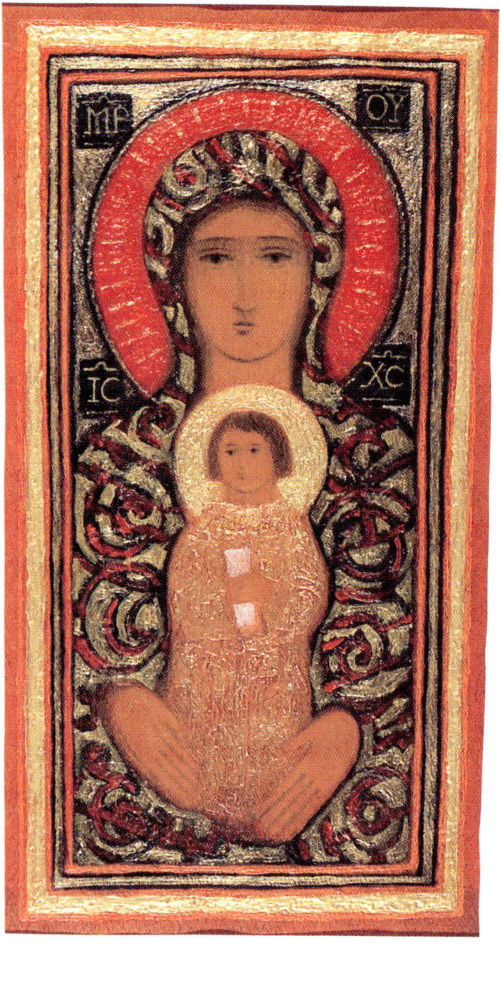
MP ΘY
IC XC

The Rosary: Method

When praying the Rosary we call to mind and meditate on fifteen events or mysteries of Christ's and Mary's lives.

Familiarity with the New Testament enhances and facilitates meditation.

While meditating we recite a prayer on each bead of the Rosary.

The Apostles' Creed is said on the crucifix; the Our Father on each of the large beads; the Hail Mary on each of the small beads; the Glory Be after the first three Hail Marys, and after each decade.

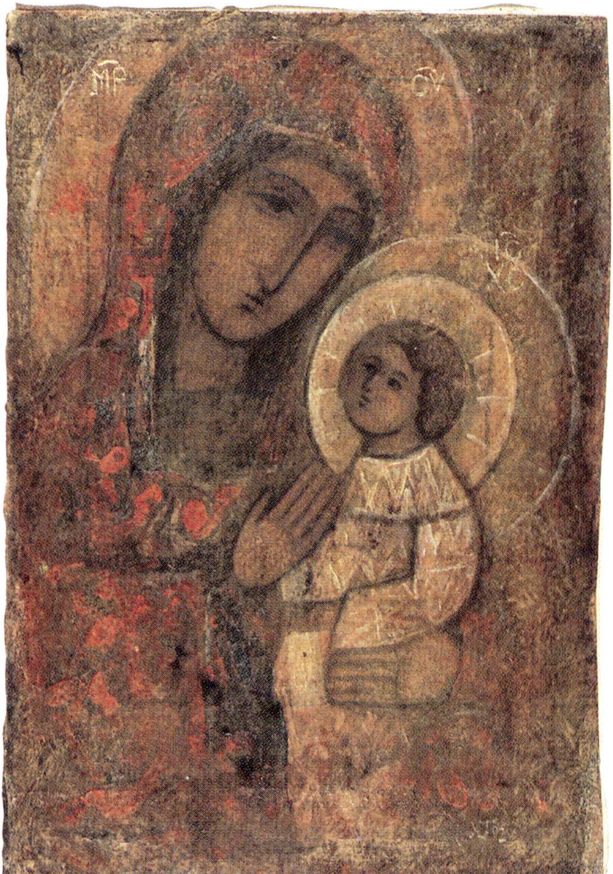

The Rosary: Mysteries

I   Joyful Mysteries:
    Annunciation
    Visitation
    Nativity
    Presentation
    Finding in the Temple

II Sorrowful Mysteries:
    Agony in the Garden
    Scourging at the Pillar
    Crowning with Thorns
    Carrying of the Cross
    Crucifixion

III Glorious Mysteries:
    Resurrection
    Ascension
    Descent of the Holy Spirit
    Assumption of Mary
    Crowning of Mary

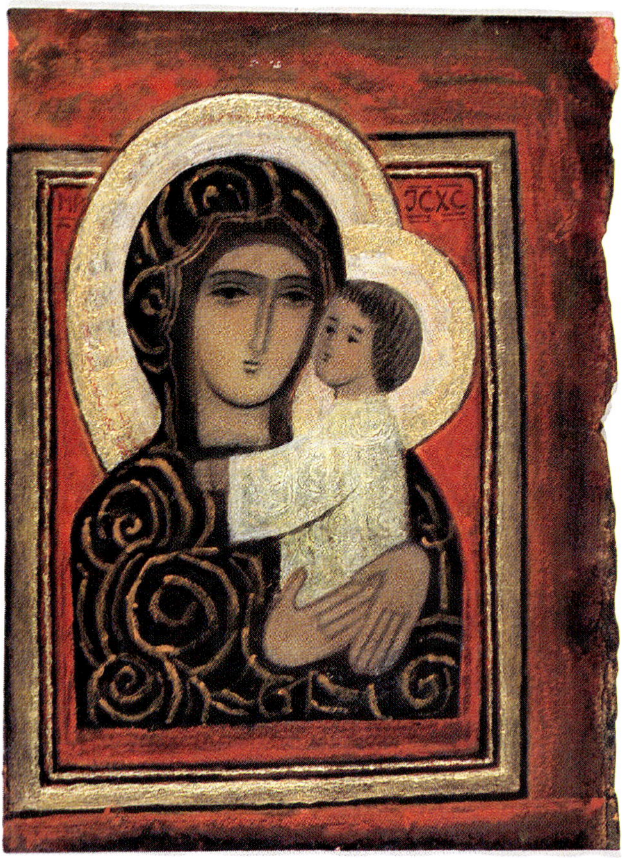
IC XC

Litany of the Blessed Virgin Mary

Lord, have mercy.
   Christ have mercy.
Lord, have mercy.
Holy Mary, pray for us.*
Holy Mother of God,
Mother of Christ,
Mother of the Church,
Mother of divine grace,
Mother most pure,
Mother most amiable,
Mother most admirable,
Mother of good counsel,
Mother of our Creator,
Mother of our Saviour,
Virgin most prudent,
Virgin most venerable,
Virgin most renowned,

* *"Pray for us" is repeated after each invocation.*

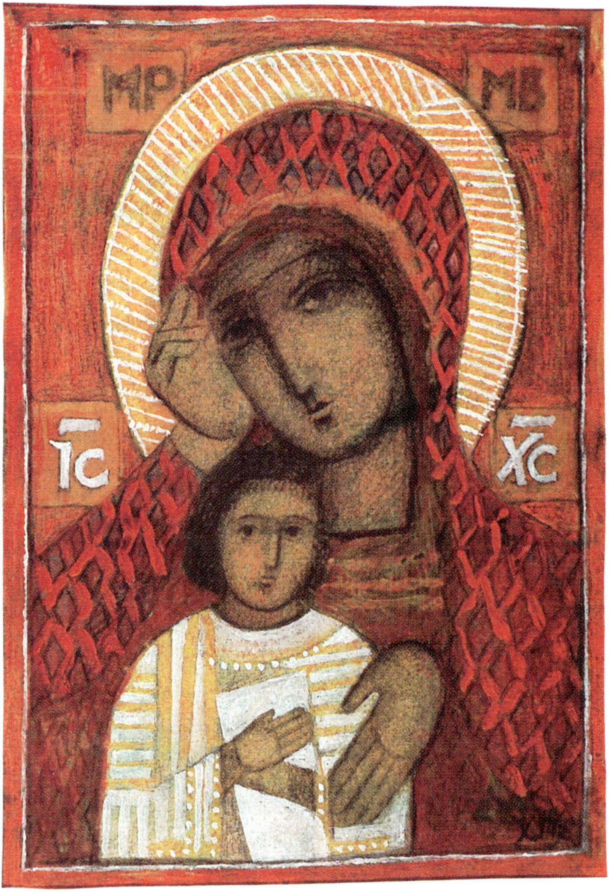

MP
MΘ
IC
XC

Virgin most powerful,
Virgin most merciful,
Virgin most faithful,
Mirror of justice,
Seat of wisdom,
Cause of our joy,
Spiritual vessel,
Vessel of honour,
Singular vessel of devotion,
Mystical rose,
Tower of David,
Tower of ivory,
House of gold,
Ark of the covenant,
Gate of heaven,
Morning star,
Health of the sick,
Refuge of sinners,

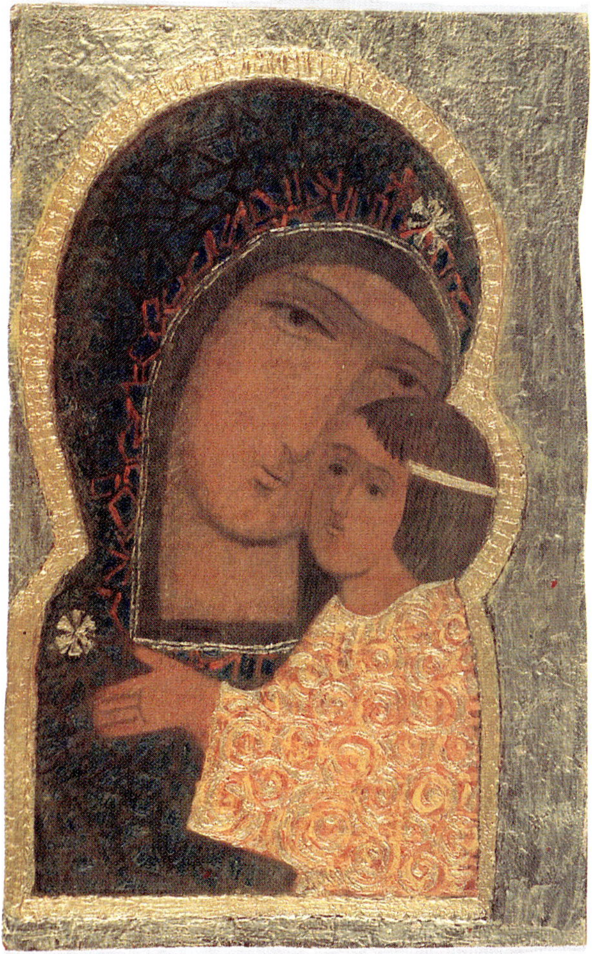

Comforter of the afflicted,
Help of Christians,
Queen of angels,
Queen of patriarchs,
Queen of prophets,
Queen of apostles,
Queen of martyrs,
Queen of confessors,
Queen of virgins,
Queen of all saints,
Queen conceived without original sin,
Queen assumed into heaven,
Queen of the most holy Rosary,
Queen of peace...
Lamb of God, you take away the sins of the world; *spare us, O Lord!*
Lamb of God, you take away the sins of the world; *graciously hear us, O Lord!*
Lamb of God, you take away the sins of the world; *have mercy on us.*

V. Pray for us, O holy Mother of God.

℟. *That we may be made worthy of the promises of Christ.*

Let us pray.
Grant, we beg You, O Lord God,
that we Your servants
may enjoy lasting health of mind and body,
and by the glorious intercession
of the Blessed Mary, ever Virgin,
be delivered from present sorrow
and enter into the joy
of eternal happiness.
Through Christ our Lord.

℟. Amen.

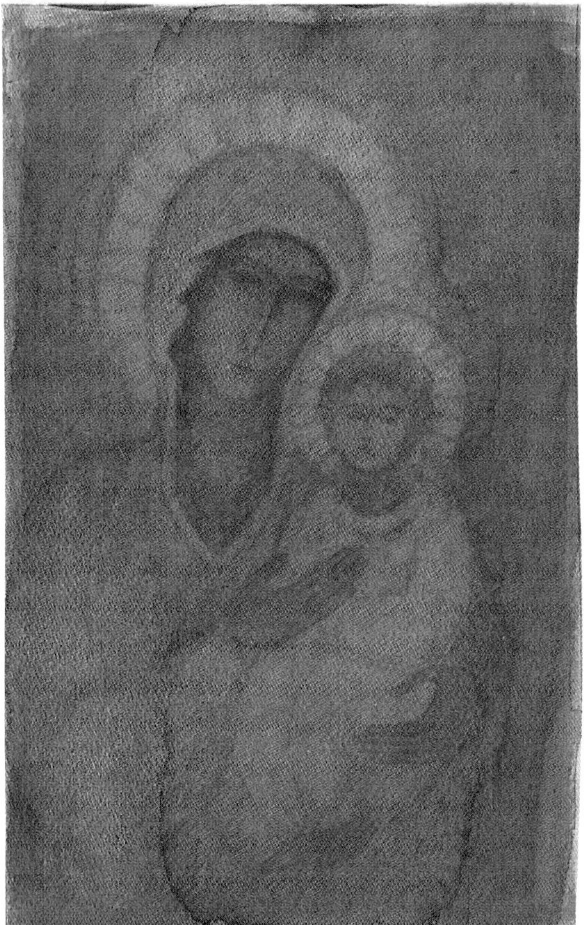

Rejoice

Rejoice, Mother of the Lamb and the Shepherd.
Rejoice, shelter for his sheep.
Rejoice, refuge from enemies unseen.
Rejoice, key that opens paradise.
Rejoice, as heaven sings with earth.
Rejoice, as earth rings out to heaven.
Rejoice, glory of the apostles.
Rejoice, strength of martyrs.
Rejoice, foundation of our faith.
Rejoice, light that leads us to God.
Rejoice, Mother-Maid!

From the Akathistos Hymn

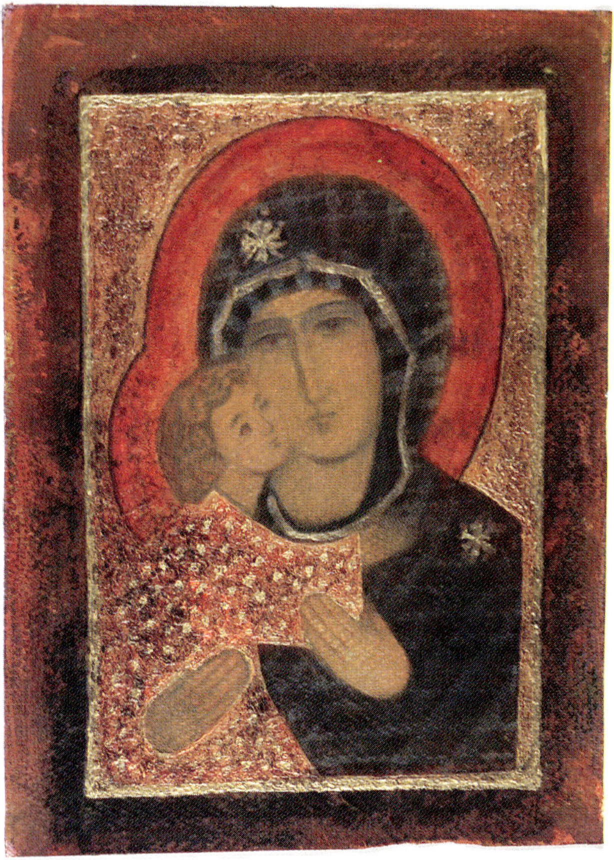

Mary, Mother of Divine Grace Compared to the Air We Breathe

Mary Immaculate,
Merely a woman, yet
Whose presence, power is
Great as no goddess's
Was deemèd, dreamèd; who
This one work has to do—
Let all God's glory through,
God's glory, which would go
Thro' her and from her flow
Off, and no way but so.

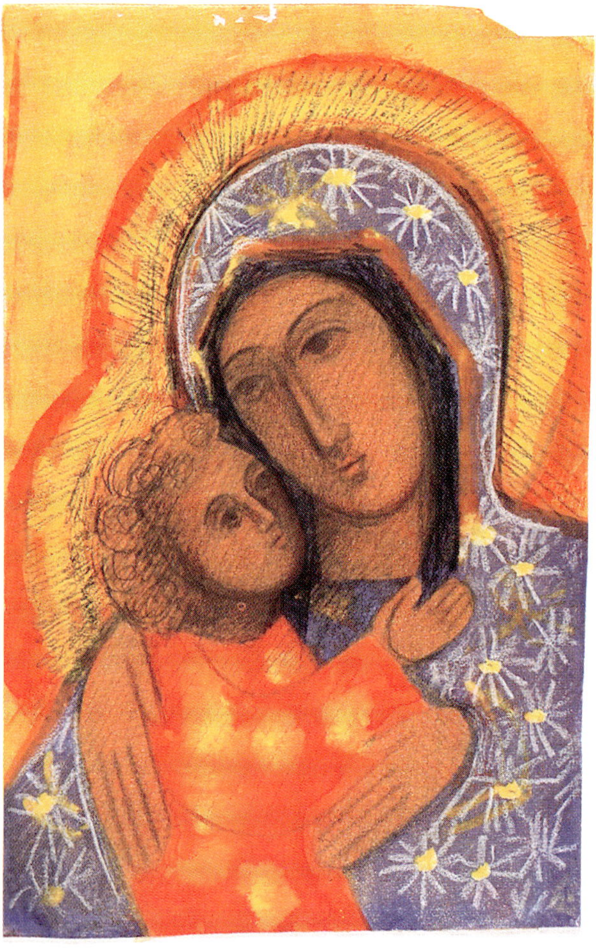

Of her flesh he took flesh:
He does take, fresh and fresh,
Though much the mystery how,
Not flesh but spirit now,
And wakes, O marvellous!
New Nazareths in us,
Where she shall yet conceive
Him, morning, noon and eve;
New Bethlems, and he born
There, evening, noon and morn.

Gerard Manley Hopkins

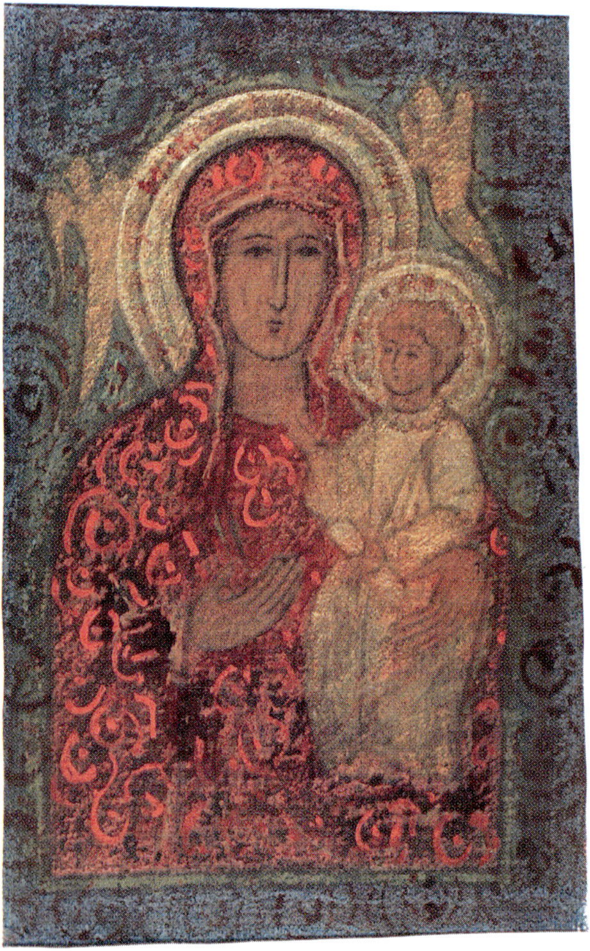

Symphonia

You never sprang from the dew,
my blossom, nor from the rain—
that was no wind that swept over you—for God's
radiance opened you
on a regal bough. On the morn
of the universe he saw you blossoming,
and he made you
a golden matrix, O maid
beyond praise, for his word.

Hildegard of Bingen

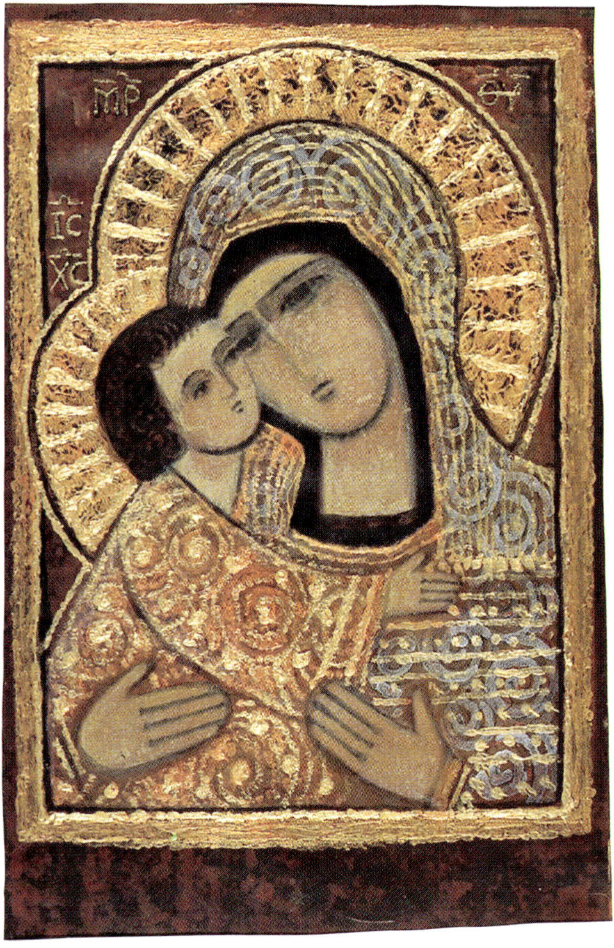
MP
ΘY
IC
XC

O First-Born Daughter

1. O first-born daughter of God's grace,
   You lead the vast array
   Of all who sing God's holy name
   Through time to endless day.

Refrain:
   Mighty God! across the spans of time
   Your mercy still we sing;
   With Mary we recall your deeds
   And joy-filled praise now bring.

2. O true disciple of the Lord,
   You call us to declare
   The deep compassion of your Son,
   God's peace beyond compare. *(Refrain)*

3. O woman, bearer of our God,
   Now midwife at the birth
   Of God's own justice, God's great day:
   The hope of all the earth. *(Refrain)*

Contemporary hymn by Bernadette Gasslein

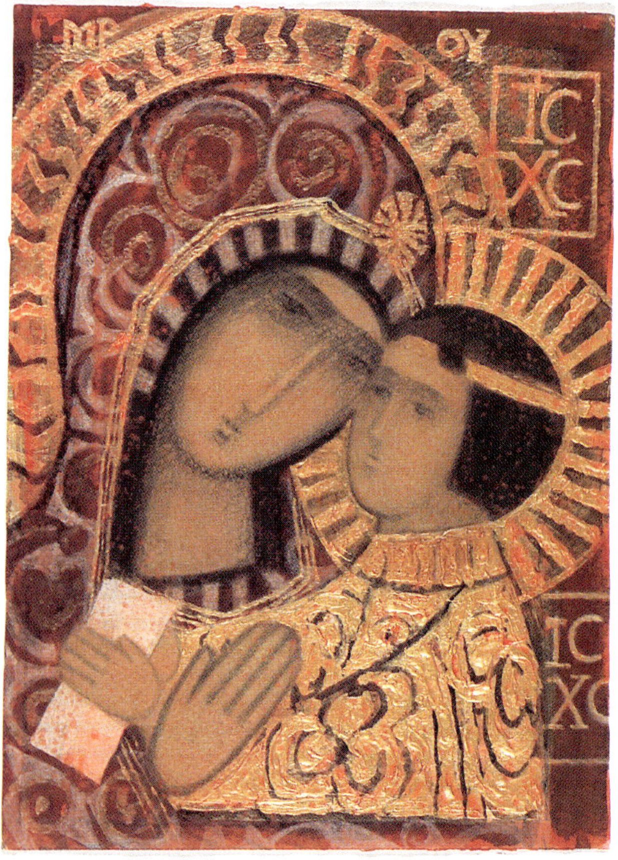
IC
XC
IC
XC

Immaculate Mary

1. Immaculate Mary, your praises we sing,
   You reign now with Jesus,
       our Saviour and King.
   Ave, ave, ave Maria,
   Ave, ave, ave Maria.

2. In heaven, the blessed
       your glory proclaim;
   On earth, we your children invoke
       your fair name.

3. Your name is our power,
       your virtues our light,
   Your love is our comfort,
       your prayers are our might.

4. We pray for the Church,
       our true mother on earth,
   And ask you to watch o'er
       the land of our birth.

Text: Anon.

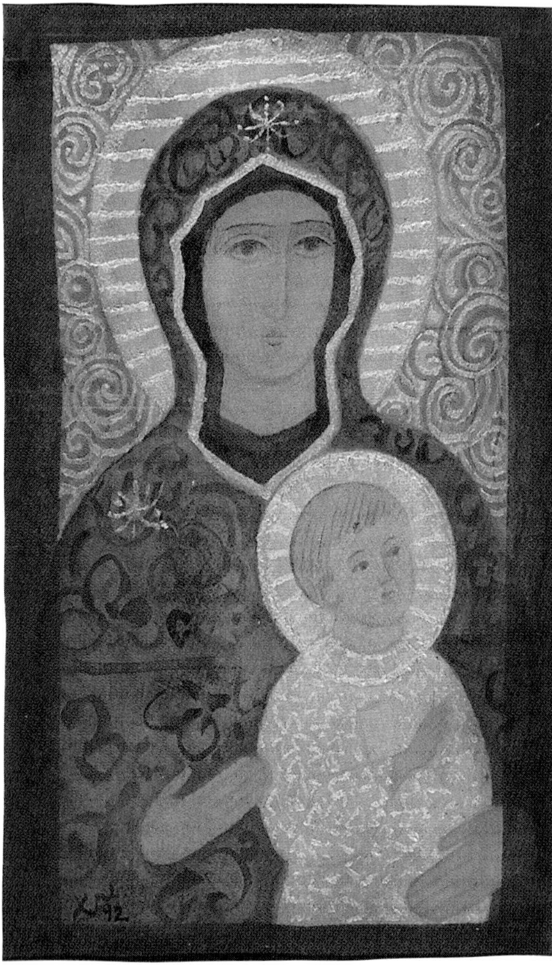

O Sanctissima

O Sanctissima,
O piissima,
Dulcis Virgo Maria!
Mater amata,
intemerata,
Ora, ora pro nobis.

Tu solatium et refugium,
Virgo mater Maria!
Quidquid optamus,
per te speramus,
Ora, ora pro nobis.

Text: 18th century

Notes

Most of the prayers in this book are traditional and were recited from memory by our parents and grandparents. Rich in poetry and theology, they deserve to be re-discovered.

The paintings reproduced in this book are either in private collections or in the possession of the artist.

P. 5: From *Julian of Norwich Showings* (Paulist Press, 1978), p. 147. Used with permission.

Pp. 9-13: © C. Granger

P. 15: One of the oldest known prayers addressed to Mary, dating from the third century. It is recited daily by many Eastern Christians. Translation: Christine Granger.

Pp. 21-23: Luke 1: 46-55. From the New Revised Standard Version of the Bible, © 1989, Division of Christian Education of the National Council of Churches of Christ in the United States. Used with permission.

P. 49: Excerpts from the Akathistos Hymn, a hymn of joy as the new creation praises Mary, the main instrument of God's redemptive plan. Translation from the Ukrainian: Christine Granger.

P. 51: From "Mary, Mother of Divine Grace Compared to the Air We Breathe," by G. M. Hopkins (1844-89). A Jesuit and poet, Hopkins was one of the most original and powerful poets in the English language.

P. 55: Reprinted from *St. Hildegard of Bingen: Symphonia: A Critical Edition of the Symphonia armonie celestium revelationum*. Edited and translated by Barbara Newman. Copyright © 1989 by Cornell University. Used by permission of the publisher, Cornell University Press.

P. 57: Copyright © 1993, Bernadette Gasslein, 1952-. Used with permission. In 1996, "O First-born Daughter" was selected as one of five prize-winning Marian texts in an international hymn search sponsored by the Mariological Society of North America.

The Paintings

I have been painting Mary since the early eighties, and continue to paint her daily. "Of Mary there is never enough," says St. Bernard, and I agree. My starting point is the Ukrainian and Byzantine icon tradition, but I consider all art, past and present, as my heritage and inspiration.

I see Mary as a gentle and gracious woman, fully in tune with God's will. She is always with her Son: she points to him, she leads us to him. I like to think of my work as an echo of Gabriel's words, "Hail Mary, full of grace, the Lord is with thee …". Each painting is a joyful reaffirmation of the mystery of the incarnation.

The artist's technique:

Although I have used various media including wax and egg tempura, I now use acrylic colours and acrylic gold. The technique of layering that I employ is widely used in iconography. Many layers or coats are applied to achieve what looks like a single colour. I like to build up textures, patterns and borders by applying paint in thick lines and layers. I love to work with reds, oranges, yellows and golds, colours usually associated with fire, light and the divine.

The mother and child image is an ancient one that goes back to pre-historic times. Perhaps that is why both believers and non-believers respond to it. Artistically, the two figures are treated as a single unit. The painting is put into the Christian context by the initials near the figures: Mary, the Mother of God and Jesus Christ.

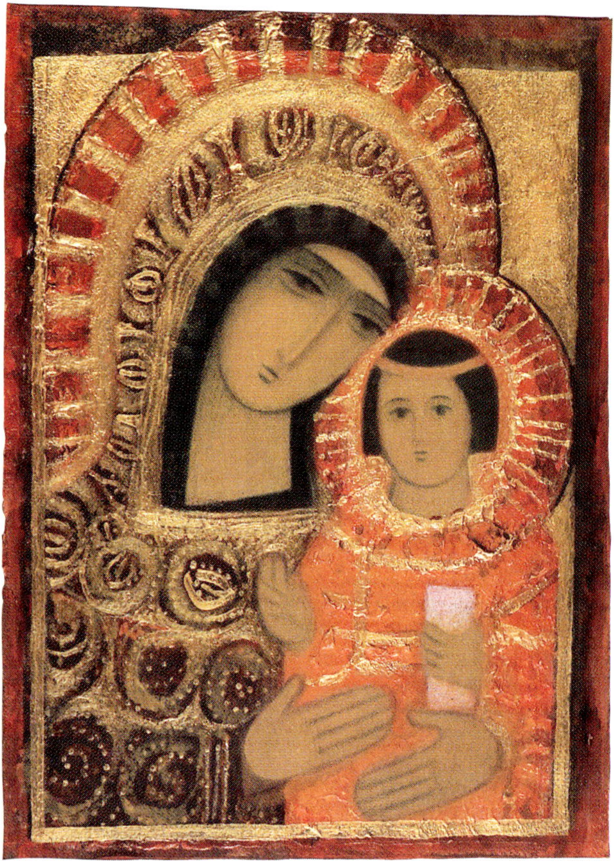